WILD READS

Sharks

Chris Powling

OXFORD
UNIVERSITY PRESS

This book belongs to:

OXFORD
UNIVERSITY PRESS

Great Clarendon Street, Oxford OX2 6DP
Oxford University Press is a department of the University of Oxford.
It furthers the University's objective of excellence in research, scholarship,
and education by publishing worldwide in

Oxford   New York

Auckland   Cape Town   Dar es Salaam   Hong Kong   Karachi
Kuala Lumpur   Madrid   Melbourne   Mexico City   Nairobi
New Delhi   Shanghai   Taipei   Toronto

With offices in

Argentina   Austria   Brazil   Chile   Czech Republic   France   Greece
Guatemala   Hungary   Italy   Japan   Poland   Portugal   Singapore
South Korea   Switzerland   Thailand   Turkey   Ukraine   Vietnam

Oxford is a registered trade mark of Oxford University Press
in the UK and in certain other countries

Text © Chris Powling
Illustrations © Rupert van Wyk
The moral rights of the author have been asserted

Database right Oxford University Press (maker)

This edition 2009

British Library Cataloguing in Publication Data

Data available

ISBN: 978-0-19-911931-8

1 3 5 7 9 10 8 6 4 2

Printed in China
Paper used in the production of this book is a natural,
recyclable product made from wood grown in sustainable forests.
The manufacturing process conforms to the environmental
regulations of the country of origin.

Contents

Sharks can be scary

Even a shark's name makes me
shiver.
It seems to be saying:

SH – to hush us

AR – to swallow us

K – to snap shut on us!

Grey reef shark

Sharks haven't changed for millions of years. They're like leftover dinosaurs.

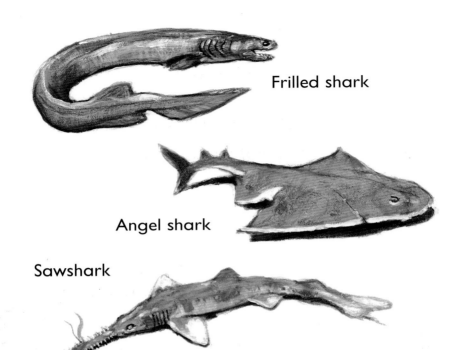

Frilled shark

Angel shark

Sawshark

Do sharks ever sleep? No.
Do sharks ever stop swimming? No.
Do sharks ever feel afraid? No.

We can say no to all these questions,
at least if we're talking about the
scariest shark of all. From the
colour of its belly, we call this the
great white.

The great white

When it's 1,000 metres away,
a great white will hear you.

When it's 500 metres away,
it'll smell you.

When it's 100 metres away,
it'll notice the splash of your feet in
the water.

Imagine being hunted by an animal that's bigger and faster than a speedboat.

What a nightmare!

Great white shark

This shark's bite is the worst part.
A great white can gulp down a
whole seal in one go. Its teeth are so
sharp you won't even feel them
slicing into you ... at first.

Other sorts of shark

Most sharks are more friendly. Look at the whale shark ...

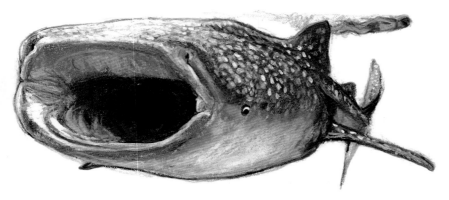

... or the basking shark.

These are the biggest fish in the sea. Amazingly, neither will harm you.

They're too busy feeding themselves.
They spend hour after hour
hoovering up tiny fish and plants.
They won't even mind if you sneak
a ride with them.

A dwarf shark, though, could sneak
a ride with you. It's the smallest
shark there is.

So far, we know about more than 350 different kinds of shark. Some are so strange, they seem almost magical. It's hard to believe in the zebra shark ...

... or the carpet shark,

... or the thresher shark.

The goblin shark is stranger still ...

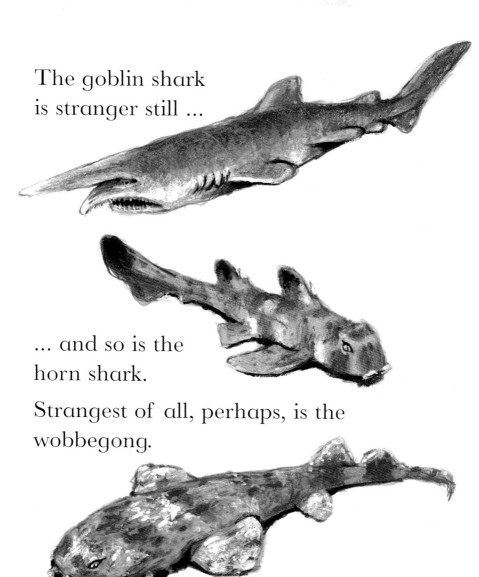

... and so is the horn shark.

Strangest of all, perhaps, is the wobbegong.

Can they all be sharks when they look so different?

How to recognize a shark

1. Check the mouth

On a shark the
mouth is tucked
under the snout.
It opens much wider
than your mouth
or mine.

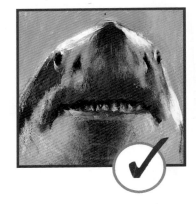

2. Check the teeth

Inside the mouth are
hundreds of teeth —
for gripping, for
crushing, for slicing.
When a tooth falls
out, another shifts
forward to take
its place.

3. Check the gills

Gills are hidden slits which help fish breath underwater. On sharks, the gills *aren't* hidden. A shark has a set of five gills on each side of its throat.

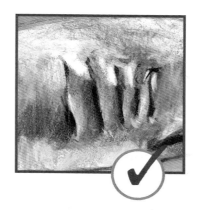

4. Check the skin ... very gently

Fish have scales but sharks are covered in tiny, tooth-like thorns called denticles. These are amazingly sharp. Stroke them one way and they'll be as smooth as silk. Stroke them the other and your fingers may gush with blood.

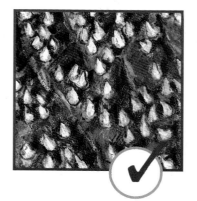

5. Check the skeleton

A shark's skeleton isn't bony. It's made of gristly stuff known as cartilage, just like your nose and your ears. That's why a shark can twist and turn so easily.

6. Check a couple of shark secrets

One is the special oil in a shark's liver that helps keep it afloat.

The other is a long, thin tube, filled with jelly. This loops from snout to tail inside a shark's body. It twangs if there's any movement in the water. Its name is the lateral line.

Are sharks really dangerous?

Well, you'd better stay on the beach if there's a great white lurking about.

Or the blue shark which swims in packs. Or the hammerhead ... the mako ... or the tiger shark

Great white

Blue shark

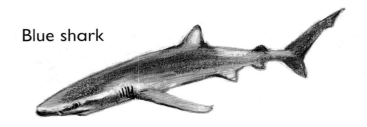

All five are sleek, skilful hunters. Mostly they kill seals, sea lions and turtles.

Hammerhead

Mako

Tiger shark

But sharks also kill people, don't they?

Only by mistake, most experts say. Sharks are so bold and so hungry, they gobble down almost anything – tin cans, old tools, plastic bags. To them, a boy or girl on a surfboard may look just like a seal or a turtle.

Remember, too, that a shark attack is very rare. There are sharks all over the world wherever the sea is warm. Yet, every year, the number of people they bite wouldn't even fill a classroom in your school.

Did you know ...
More people are
struck by lightning
than bitten by sharks!

▶ A shark's worst enemy

This may surprise you. Human beings are far more deadly to sharks than sharks are to us!

We hunt them for sport.

We turn their teeth into necklaces.

We use their skin for shoes and wallets and handbags.

We crush their skeleton for plant food.

We even take the oil in their liver for making perfume and face cream and soap.

BAMBOO PALACE MENU

Supreme Broth
Tiger Sharkfin Soup
Dark Chicken Sharkfin Soup
Crab Meat Sharkfin Soup
Boiled Dried Seafood Deluxe
Roast Duck in Plum Sauce
Squid in Black Bean Sauce
Steamed Vegetables with
Oyster Sauce
Egg Fried Rice
Jasmine Tea

Also, we eat them … in sharkfin soup
for starters and as steaks for a main
course. If you like fish and chips,
watch out for "huss" or "rock
salmon" on the menu. Its real name
is the dogfish. And that's a small
shark.

The vanishing shark

Sharks are beginning to disappear.

Nowadays we kill sharks much faster than they can breed. In fact, we don't know much about how sharks have babies. Or how often it happens.

Some sharks lay eggs in a special case called a mermaid's purse.

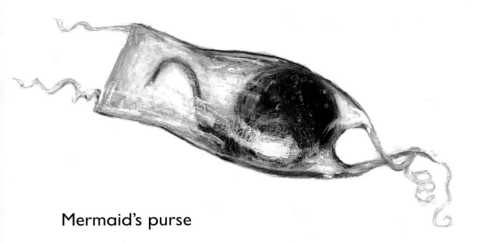

Mermaid's purse

Other sharks are hatched inside their mother. A lemon shark is different again – it gives birth to a pup that's nearly as big as a man.

These babies have always been easy food for bigger sea creatures.

Eventually, if we're not careful, there may not be any sharks left in the sea.

Think about that.

Lemon shark and pup

Do we really want sharks to die out altogether just like dinosaurs?

Of course, I wouldn't want a shark as a pet. Would you? But I'd love to discover more about them. How much food do they really eat, for instance? And how long do they live? Even shark experts can't answer these questions yet.

Great white sharks

Maybe we should find a new way of saying their name. Why not try:

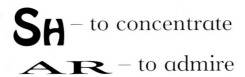

SH – to concentrate

AR – to admire

K – to click the camera for a close-up.

That should do it!

Greenland shark

Leopard shark

Bull shark

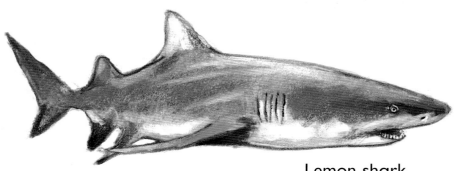

Lemon shark

Sharks still send a shiver
up my spine.
But I hope these mysterious creatures
will always be there to scare us and
thrill us.

▶ Glossary

 breed When sharks breed they produce babies. **24**

 cartilage Sharks have a skeleton made of tough but elastic material called cartilage. **16**

 denticles Denticles are the little sharp scales that cover a shark's body. **15**

 gills Gills are the long thin slits behind a shark's head. The shark uses them to breathe through. **15**

lateral line The lateral line is a long, thin tube, filled with jelly. This loops from snout to tail inside a shark's body. It twangs if there's any movement in the water. **17**

 mermaid's purse Some sharks lay their eggs in a mermaid's purse. It is a little bag that protects a shark's eggs. **24**

 pup A pup is a baby shark. **25**

 snout A snout is the pointed "nose" in front of a shark's eyes. **14, 17**

OXFORD

WILD READS

WILD READS will help your child develop a love of reading and a lasting curiosity about our world. See the websites and places to visit below to learn more about sharks.

Sharks

WEBSITES

http://www.wwf.org.uk/gowild/index.asp

http://www.londonaquarium.co.uk/conservation-education-London-Aquarium
Adopt a shark at the London Aquarium.

http://www.bbc.co.uk/cbbc/wild/

PLACES TO VISIT

Chessington World of Adventure – Sea Life centre.
http://www.chessington.com/
Take a walk through an ocean tank while sharks swim over your head!

Whale, Dolphin, Shark and Wildlife Watch with Sea Life Surveys, Scotland.
http://www.sealifesurveys.com/
See sharks in their natural habitat.

The Natural History Museum
http://www.nhm.ac.uk/index.html